To Selah, Elijah, and Judah.
Continue to shine brilliantly and beautifully. —M.O.
For Judah. —C.B.

Before the Ships

The Birth of Black Excellence

Written by
Maisha Oso

Illustrated by
Candice Bradley

Orchard Books
An imprint of Scholastic Inc.
New York

Long before a slave ship sailed,
we shined like stars —
brilliant and beautiful.

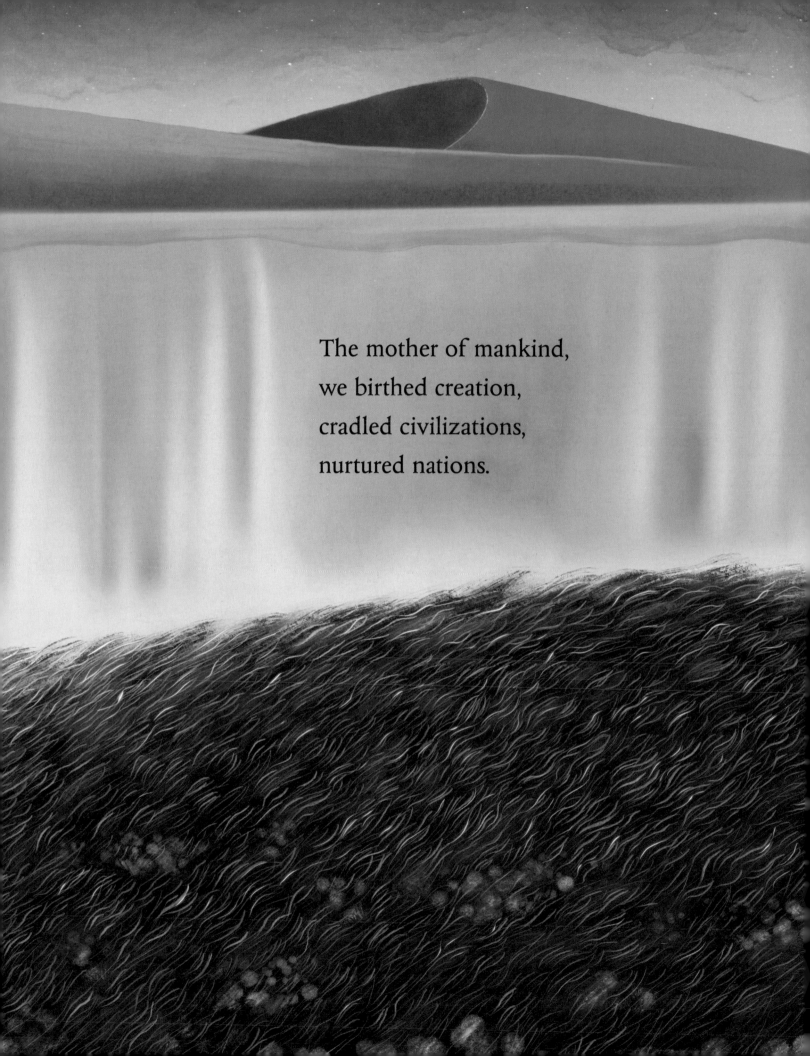

The mother of mankind,
we birthed creation,
cradled civilizations,
nurtured nations.

In Africa, we were royalty,
reigning, ruling entire empires.
Kings and queens of great renown
in shades of brown — just like you.

We were doctors, farmers, leaders of tribes,
merchants, miners, artisans, scribes.
Our heads held high, we beamed with pride
before the ships.

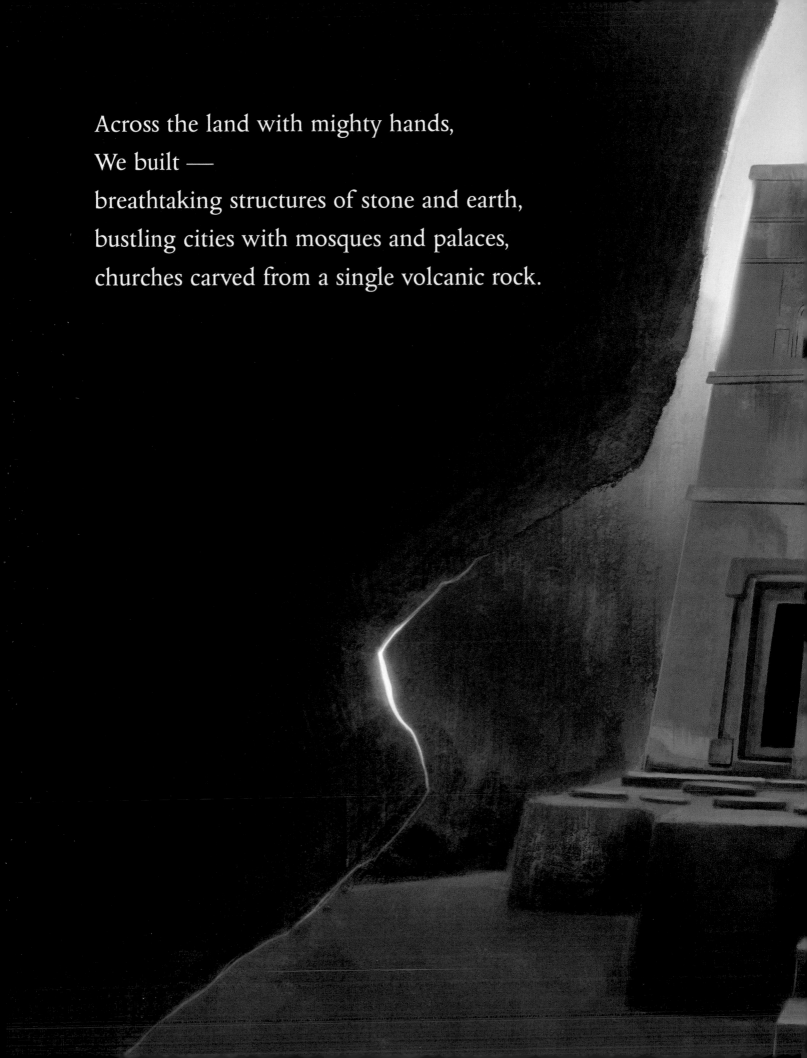

Across the land with mighty hands,
We built —
breathtaking structures of stone and earth,
bustling cities with mosques and palaces,
churches carved from a single volcanic rock.

In those days, we were warriors —
willing to battle anything that got in our way.
From Hannibal, the great general of Carthage,
to Amanirenas, the warrior queen of Kush,
we fought fiercely in the armies of ancient Africa.

Before the first ship left the shore, we learned from lore.
Griots shared stories in song. Koras were strummed to
beating drums as Hausa history and Fulani folktales were
passed down through generations.

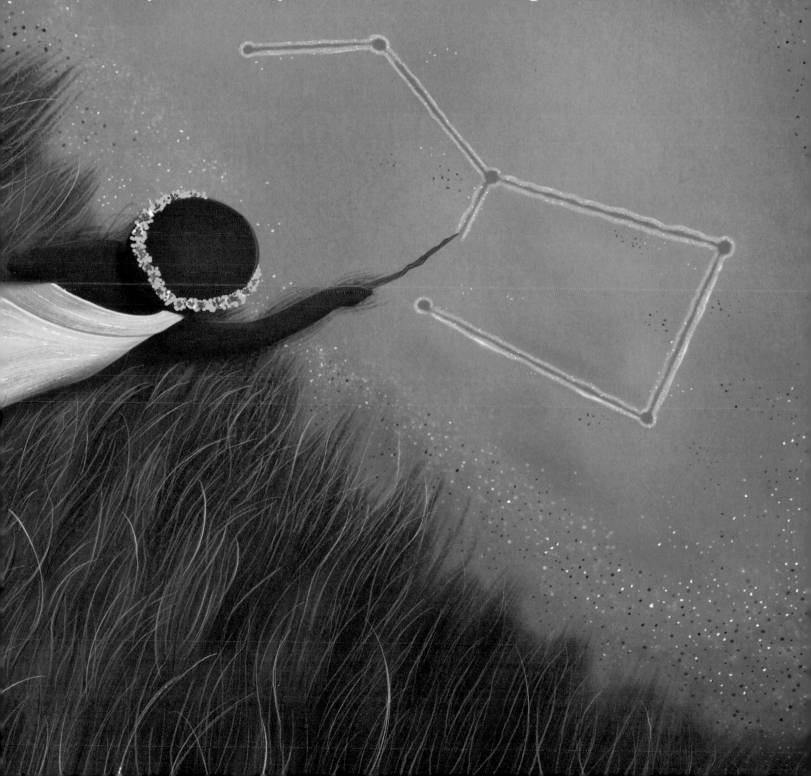

On the grasslands of the Mara and the sands of the Sahara,
we dreamed —
Our magical minds uncovering the mysteries of the galaxy.
From mathematics, to astronomy, to engineering,
many modern-day sciences *stem* from our genius.

Here we stand, after the ships,
as amazing as we've always been.
Still daring to dream the impossible.
Unstoppable, we continue to tell our stories,
showing the world that Black lives
have always mattered.

We are still warriors —
Fighting for freedom and fairness.
We're fearless, courageous competitors,
excelling in every space we enter.

$$a = 2, \ b = -4, \ \text{and} \ c = -30$$

$$x = \frac{-b \pm \sqrt{b^2 - 4ac}}{2a}$$

$$x = \frac{4 \pm \sqrt{-4^2 - 4 \times 2 \times -30}}{2 \times 2}$$

$$x = \frac{4 \pm \sqrt{16 + 240}}{4}$$

$$x = \frac{4 \pm \sqrt{256}}{4}$$

$$x_1 = \frac{4 + 16}{4} = 5$$

We are born leaders.
We're regal and skilled,
still proud as we build
a better future for those yet to come.

$$\frac{4 \pm 16}{4}$$

$$x_2 = \frac{4 - 16}{4} = ?$$

We are
still shining,
still beautiful,
still brilliant.
Like diamonds under pressure,
we are precious and resilient.

We're the stars that rise to
grace the skies,
illuminating the night.
We sparkle bright.

We are the light.

Author's Note

I was born and raised in New York City where my public school education in Black history began with slavery and ended with the civil rights movement. For the longest time, I wondered about the impact of teaching young children that they are descendants of *slaves* without exploring the rich history that came before their enslavement: a beautiful history of Africans that is too often overlooked in studies of world history.

In 2013, I moved to Africa for an international assignment. Over the next several years, I went on to live in two different countries on the continent and travel to several more. I visited the Rock-Hewn Churches of Lalibela, Ethiopia; immersed myself in the arts and consumed the cuisine of Johannesburg, South Africa; spent mornings in the Masai Mara in Kenya; and tackled some of the teeming markets of Lagos, Nigeria. I know that Africa is not a monolith. Its people are dynamic and diverse, but from coast to coast, they share a strength, ingenuity, and resilience that deserve to be marveled at.

I wrote *Before the Ships* to tell their story, and by doing so, to tell ours. I wrote it to let countless children know that Black history does not begin with slavery — that before they were bound, they were free. I wrote this story to show children that the same strength, ingenuity, and resilience that existed before run through their veins right now — and that's why we shine like stars — brilliant and beautiful.

— Maisha Oso